ABOVE: *The Gardener, an illustration from 'The Book of English Trades and Library of the Useful Arts' (London, 1824). While the reader may question this well dressed gentleman in his well tended garden digging in the middle of the lawn, it must be accepted that the spade, rake, watering can, halfmoon blade and flowerpots vary little from today's designs.*

OPPOSITE: *An advertisement from a late Victorian trade journal.*

OLD GARDEN TOOLS

Kay N. Sanecki

Shire Publications Ltd

CONTENTS

Printed in Great Britain by C. I. Thomas & Sons (Haverfordwest) Ltd, Press Buildings, Merlins Bridge, Haverfordwest.

ACKNOWLEDGEMENTS

The author is indebted to many museum keepers and their staff for giving their time and answering so many questions. Special thanks are due to David C. Phillips, Archivist, Museum of English Rural Life, University of Reading. The author would like also to acknowledge the work of Sandra Raphael on Evelyn's *Elysium Britannicum* and of Dennis Parrish on lawnmowers at the Museum of English Rural Life.

Illustrations are acknowledged as follows: Buckinghamshire County Museum, pages 3, 16-17, 22, 23; the Iris Hardwick Library of Photographs, pages 7, 12, 13, 18 (bottom), 26 (upper and lower right), 30; Museum of English Rural Life, University of Reading, pages 1, 9 (top), 10, 14, 18 (top), 19, 20, 21, 24, 25, 26 (left), 27, 28, 29, 31, 32, and inside front cover.

ABOVE: *Detail of a painting by Balthazar Nebot of Hartwell House, Buckinghamshire, showing gardeners with scythes, c. 1738.*

GARDEN TOOLS OF THE PAST

Some of the oldest implements in the world are those that have been used for the cultivation of the land. The basic shapes of tools such as spades, picks and knives have changed little since Roman times, refinement of design and improvement of materials being the main differences. Local design, sometimes made even to a personal preference, persisted well into the middle of the twentieth century and it is only since the Second World War that standardisation has become apparent and, it would seem, acceptable.

Like most craftsmen, gardeners have been inventive and sometimes personally designed tools are to be found, probably blacksmith-made to the individual requirement.

During the seventeenth century, when there was an intense interest in horticultural practice, more specialised equipment became available. Then, following the industrial revolution, gardening became the leisure occupation of so many new middle-class town dwellers that the manufacture of garden implements and the mechanisation of mowers began. The general picture shows that between the two world wars in the twentieth century there was a variety of design in any and every piece of garden equipment such as had not been seen before. This trend has not persisted. Tools have become standardised, mainly to meet the demands of long production runs to make the manufacture economical.

Many tools of the past have been such commonplace commodities that they have not been preserved and little remains now to be seen that predates the Victorian era, except in one or two specialised collections.

Two pages from John Evelyn's 'Elysium Britannicum' (1659), described on page 6.

An eighteenth-century book plate, published in both France and London, used in 'Le Jardinier Solitaire' ('The Solitary or Carthusian Gardener') by Francis Gentil (London, 1706), depicts tools and the accompanying caption reads:

1. Spade. The first instrument the Gardener takes in his hand. It is chiefly used by Apprentices.

2. Shovel. Used for throwing earth out of a Trench or Ditch to throw rakings into a wheelbarrow or Dosser.

3. Rakes. This tool, is in the Gardener's Trade, a symbol of Neatness.

4. Rakers. A necessary tool for keeping the Garden clean of weeds.

5. Displanter. Used for transplanting, and for taking up all Flowers, that the Gardener is obliged to transplant from the place where they were sowed to another.

6. Pruning knife. So necessary, that a Gardener ought always to have one in his pocket.

7. Dibbles. For planting small Flowers that have roots and for planting Bulbs.

8. Watering Pot. It imitates the rain, falling from the Heavens.

9. Beetle. This serves to smooth the Walks and hinders most effectively the growing of Weeds upon 'em.

10. Flower Basket. A Gardener that cultivates Flowers ought to have Baskets by him, to gather the Flowers in upon occasion. This sort of Basket, shew a Gardener's Neatness and the genteel way of his Profession.

11. Sieve. Tis by this that the Earth is reduced almost to Dust.

12. Saw. For cutting the Branches which can't be lopped with a knife.

13. Transplanter. Used for raising together with the earth, plants for transplanting.

14. Garden Pot. To put Flowers in, that grow better so than in full earth, such as Pinks, Bear-Ears, Tube-roses, etc. These may be either of plain Earth, or of Dutch Ware, the former are much larger, for holding Jassamine and Clove-Gill-flowers.

15. Plainer, or Rabot. Tho' you run the Rake never so often along the Walks and Paths — it will leave some roughness, which is easily rectified with this instrument.

16. Paillassons, or Panniers of Straw. Very necessary to keep out the Frost.

17. Mallet. Used with a chizzel for lopping Branches that can't be so neatly taken off with the force of ones hand.

18. Wheelbarrow. To carry the Stones and Rakings of Garden to Places

PREVIOUS PAGES: *About 1659 John Evelyn was writing his 'Elysium Britannicum', and the illustrations on pages 4 and 5 depict the tools and equipment he detailed as being necessary. Reading from the top down page 4 and then down page 5: iron-clad spades, rakes, hoes, pickaxe and shovel; sieves and screens and instruments peculiar to the surveyor; lines, dibbers, transplanter and a 'planting lattice . . . for regular planting and setting of rootes and flowers . . .'; ladder, trowels, turf lifter, turf edger, scythe, slasher and trowel; stone roller, leveller, tamper, funnel, hoe; shears and long pruners; slashers, knives, hammers, mattocks and pliers; ladder, and three different designs of watering pots; water barrel, water tanks and fountains; forcing pots, protection cone, frame, bell glasses; hand light bedstead 'furnished with tester and Curtaines of Greene' . . . to draw over and preserve the Choysest flowers, being in their beauty, from the parching beames of the Sunn'; knife sharpener, barrows; baskets, bird scarers (bells), storage chest, garden diary or register, and traps.*

A book plate from 'Le Jardinier Solitaire', published in London in 1706. The original caption is reproduced in the text on pages 6 and 8.

appointed to receive 'em; or, to carry Earth, or Mould, to improve such Grounds as are hungry.

19. Handbarrow. To carry into the Green-house, Trees or Shrubs, set in boxes. . .Tis like wise of use for carrying Dung upon the Beds.

20. Caterpillar Shears. For removing Caterpillars which would otherwise destroy all. They clip, or cut the end of the Branch upon which the Tuft of Caterpillars is lodg'd.

21. Garden Shears. For trimming the Box, Yews and other Trees and Shrubs that serve to embellish a Garden.

22. Double Ladder. For trimming the upper part of an Arbour, or high Bower.

23. Pickaxe. For raising the Plants that adorn the Borders. . .or for giving some small Culture to Trees and Shrubs.

24. Rolling Stone. For smoothing Walks after they are raked.

25. Hook. A Gardener that has Rows of Greens to dress, can't trim them well without a Hook, which is used after a certain way.

26. Glass Bell. A Florist can't be without this unless he has a mind to run the risk of losing his Plants, such as are soon in Beds immediately after the end of Winter.

27. Straw Bell. Proper for covering Plants newly transplanted, in order to guard them from the Heat or the Sun, which might annoy them at first.

28. Garden Fork. For spreading and disposing of Dung upon the Beds.

29. Trowel. By the help of which a Flower Gardener takes up Plants with Earth about them.

30. Hurdle. For passing the Earth through. Of great use for separating the good Earth from the Stones.

In this caption Francis Gentil not only names the tools but offers an interesting insight into the numerous gardening operations. Generally, they are the same today but for the advent of chemical insecticides, mechanical hedge trimmers, plastic sheeting and cloches — and gardening can be carried on successfully without such modern devices.

Numerous books of the seventeenth and eighteenth centuries include lists of tools 'necessary to the gardener' and it was not until the mid nineteenth century that manufacturers' catalogues replaced and extended the lists of necessary equipment. By then gardening was becoming the preoccupation of the middle classes as a leisure activity, and the immense array of gardening equipment was considered an adjunct to the Victorian villa home.

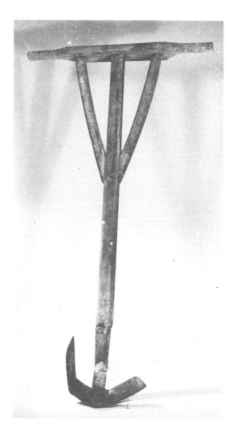

CULTIVATION

In the past, before land could be cultivated the surface layer of turf containing the weeds and insect pests had to be removed. On a small scale a pickaxe or spade could break up the land or the surface turf could be skimmed off in a process known in many areas as velling, then ripped away or rolled back, collected and burned. The ashes then provided good soil-improving material to be returned to the land. This process was often known as a 'slash and burn' cultivation.

On a large scale, for estate work or market gardening, the breast plough or breast spade was used. The latter name is preferable because the implement is in no way a plough. Paring spades served the same purpose; in Scotland they were called flaughters and varied only slightly in construction and design. The names varied also from one area to another, as push plough, spinning plough (or plow), or paring shovel.

The method of operation was always the same, the blade being thrust forward in jerks against the turf or sod by the force of the body. The implement was pushed from the thighs or lower waist and not by the chest as might be supposed. (The word 'breast' has been shown to be a dialect word for a slice or turf-cut.) Sometimes boards, or 'beaters' or 'clappers', were strapped to the front of the worker's thighs to resist the inevitable jolting action. The work must have been extremely tough, but the use of the breast spade persisted into the early years of the twentieth century.

The necessity to clear land has always existed, and there is evidence of simple paring tools in the thirteenth century. Gervais Markham, to whom many garden historians turn for information, in *Farewell to Husbandry* (1684) depicts a paring spade shaped like an arrowhead

and with a short shaft. Earlier in the same century Hartlib described an instrument 'sharp on both sides, which a man, with violence, thrusts before him'. Various designs of turf lifters and parers were evolved, most of them blacksmith-made during the seventeenth and eighteenth centuries.

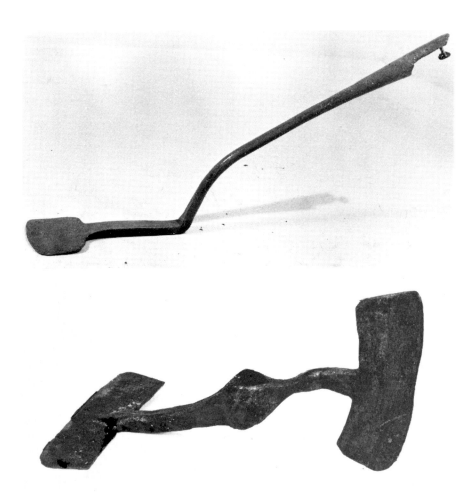

TOP: *An iron turf lifter, used for clearing surface land on a small scale, that is horticulturally. The thigh was pushed against the upper part of the curved handle in a series of thrusts to strip back the surface growth.*

ABOVE: *The head of a blacksmith-made turf lifter or paring iron. One blade was used to break up the turf into sections and the other to scrape back or lift the mat of grass and weed.*

Early spades were iron-shod. While the basic design has remained the same since ancient times, materials have improved, rendering the tool lighter to handle and more useful as a chopping implement. Turf lifters have therefore fallen into disuse. Spades were relatively common in Roman Britain; their iron cladding or sheaths have survived in numerous instances. A delightful carving depicting a monk with a wooden iron-shod spade, is to be seen on the misericord of the Dean's stall in Lincoln Cathedral.

As long as the spade remained heavy and cumbersome it was necessary to have a variety of hacking or chopping implements to loosen root-bound soil or to break up compacted earth, and a whole range of mattocks and two-pronged picks,

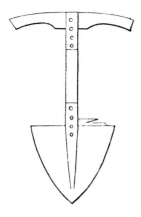

The under-foot spade (as opposed to the breast spade) described by J. C. Loudon in his 'Encyclopaedia of Gardening' (1824). The blade was about 14 inches (360 mm) wide and 12 inches (300 mm) deep, pointed and absolutely perpendicular in line with the stout handle. It was described thus: 'For the stubbing of hedges, taking the top sods off drains and various uses where strength is wanted, this spade will be found a most powerful instrument.' This is a design intermediate between the garden spade of today and the breast spade of previous centuries.

the prongs set at right angles to the handle, can be found. From these have evolved the claw-like cultivators of today on the one hand and the hoes on the other.

Local predilection for special spade design survived well into the middle of the twentieth century and still does to a certain extent. Nowadays spade design has become standardised because of the use of new materials such as plastics and aluminium, both of which are diecast rather than forged, and because ease of manufacture demands longer production runs. But old loyalties die hard and regional designs, which have been favoured for more than a hundred years, are still to be found.

The traditional digging tool of Devon, Cornwall and west Wales is a distinctive 'shovel' with a pointed, roughly triangular blade and a 'long knob' shaft. Sometimes

an indentation is carved away (even by the owner) to afford a grip for the hand, and the action is to rest the centre of the shaft on the knee to provide the fulcrum of lift. Spades of this design are still used in that area, but partly because many retired people live there the popularity of the modern stainless steel and plastic standardised digging spade has increased.

Long handles have been favoured also in Lincolnshire but usually with the standard rectangular blade without tread and with T handle. A treaded blade was in greater demand in areas on heavy soils where more thrust with the foot was needed, as on the London clay. A treaded spade invariably also had a D handle. The D handle was always preferred in the north of England, where heavy boots or clogs were used by the artisans, but not in Scotland.

Local spade shapes: 1 traditional 'shovel' from Devon, Cornwall and Wales; 2 long-handled spade from Lincolnshire; 3 northern version with shorter handle; 4 midland spade with D handle; 5 D-handled spade with tread, popular in the south-east of England.

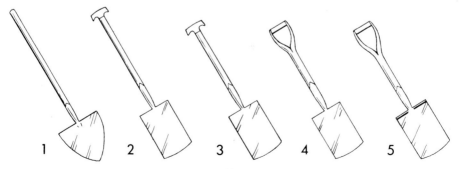

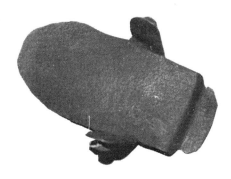

ABOVE: *A digging shoe, an iron plate strapped to the boot, was often worn on the thrusting foot to prevent damage by the spade blade to the leather sole of the boot. These were not used so much in areas where clogs, complete with clog irons, were worn.*

TOP RIGHT: *A blacksmith-made spade, such as was made in village forges before the industrial revolution and indeed for many years after. The size and shape could be adjusted to individual requirements. Such tools were usually socketed rather than strapped to attach the handle to the blade. Socketed tools are easier to handle and re-handle: the only painstaking task is to scrape away the butt of the old wooden handle and an amateur can insert a new shaft. But tubular sockets were much more likely to cause breakage at the point where the shaft enters the socket. Strapped sockets, usually with three rivets, provide a more flexible spade (or fork) less susceptible to breakage.*

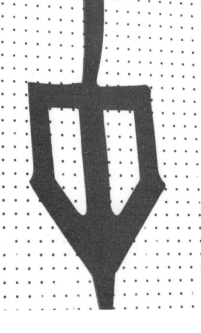

BELOW RIGHT: *Some spade blades were much narrower, designed for drainage work or for digging in wet soils. Others were adapted with open blades, as shown, and known as mules. These were lighter to handle and therefore much easier to work with on wet or very sticky soils. Most of them were blacksmith-made, but there were some manufactured designs early in the twentieth century. Note that while the shape harks back to the breast-spade blade, the general design is nearer to the garden fork.*

12

RIGHT: *A flat-tined fork, blacksmith-made with socket and therefore far less flexible than the modern round-tined garden fork with strapped joint between tines and shaft and tines of stainless steel. Flat-tined forks were used as digging tools, especially for breaking up ground previously worked over with a spade or for breaking up soil in the base of a trench. More recently the flat-tined fork was reserved for lifting potatoes and carrots and other root crops, for it was much less likely to damage the tubers or roots.*

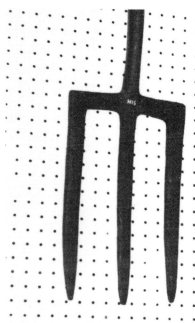

BELOW: *The trowel (left), invented in the seventeenth century, consisted of a long semi-circular piece of metal with a handle, forming a hand tool. It had been developed from the planter which is shown on page 7 (item 13) and called a transplanter. It remained much the same in design until about the 1830s. The blade then was still curved and remained so until after the First World War. The hand fork (right) is essentially a weeding tool used for close work. There is no strong evidence to show that it has been used through the centuries, though a small tool like this might easily not have survived.*

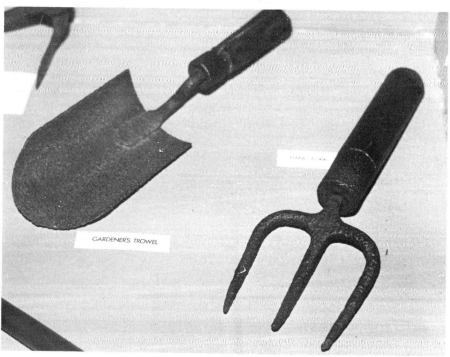

GARDENER'S TROWEL

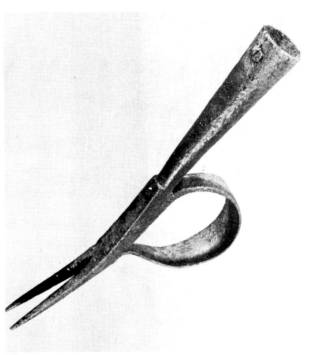

ABOVE LEFT AND RIGHT: *Forerunners of the hand fork were weeders such as these. The prongs were worked around the weeds and would lift a plant complete with root in all but hard dry soil. The balls afforded leverage on the adjacent ground. The stouter (above right) was probably used to tackle docks or thistles, as considerably more leverage could be obtained. The smaller (above left) is illustrated in some old books as a daisy grubber. Several designs of weeding tools are to be seen in museum collections. Some of them resemble long-handled pincers, sometimes with ribbed surfaces to the head to increase grip; these were thistlers.*

LEFT: *Planting tools of varying design were used to form a hole into which a seed, bulb or tuber could be put. This tool, from Oxfordshire, generally accepted as a bulb planter, may well have served also as a potato planter. By thrusting with the foot on the cross piece, a core of earth could be removed from quite solid banks or turf for bulb planting, or in rows for potato planting.*

CUTTING TOOLS

Illustrations in gardening books of the past give the impression that gardeners were obsessed with knives, saws and other cutting instruments for clipping, pruning and training trees and shrubs.

By the time specialised cutting instruments like those illustrated below were being made in Sheffield a whole range of pruners was available. Some had long handles and it was claimed that the operation of cutting through a branch 1½ inches (38mm) in diameter could be carried out with one hand. Some were claimed to leave the twig as cleanly cut as the removed pruning, and others were especially designed for ladies and for more delicate operations such as gathering bunches of grapes.

Cutting instruments as depicted in Loudon's 'Encyclopaedia of Gardening', written in the 1820s: (from top, left to right) scythe; turf shears; verge shears; two pairs of hedge shears; Dutch long-handled pruning shears; three types of pruning shears; pruning shears also suitable for gathering grapes; an averruncator (long-handled pruning instrument).

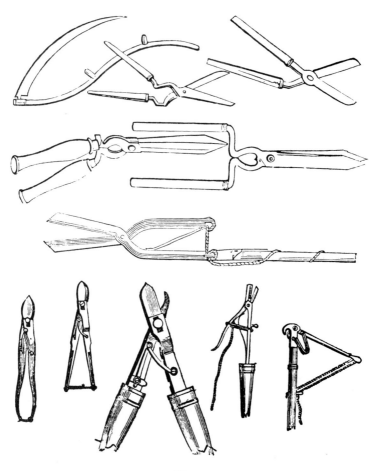

16

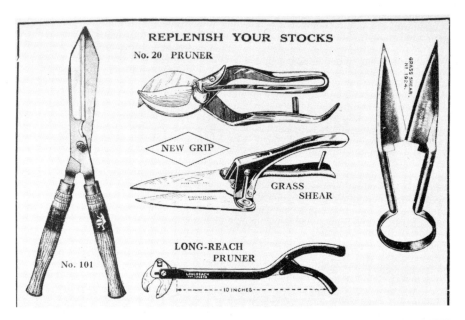

REPLENISH YOUR STOCKS

No. 20 PRUNER

NEW GRIP

GRASS SHEAR

No. 101

LONG-REACH PRUNER

10 INCHES

GRASS SHEAR. No. 1924.

ABOVE: *Shears became slightly lighter, though still with wooden handles. Grass hand shears (right) were of the age-old design, but turf shears or grass shears (centre) were redesigned for ease of operation. Long-handled pruners (below) were also slightly modified but were still heavy instruments.*

RIGHT: *Pruning scissors, as shown at the extreme left of the scissor range in the illustration opposite.*

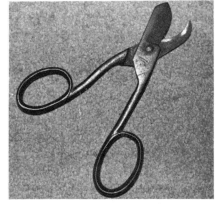

PREVIOUS PAGES: *One of the paintings by Nebot (dealt with in more detail on page 23) of Hartwell House, Buckinghamshire. A gardener trims the tall formal hedges with hand shears. Another sweeps up and collects the trimmings while a third rolls the fine gravel walk.*

HORTICULTURAL REQUISITES.

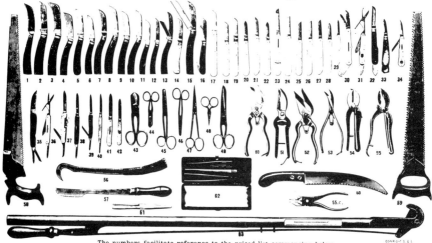

The numbers facilitate reference to the priced list commencing below.

KNIVES, SCISSORS, PRUNERS &c.

No.					Each s. d.
1	**Sheath Pruning Knife**, superior finish, does not close				2 6
2	**Pruning Knife**, large size				3 6
3	,,	,,			3 3
4	,,	,,	medium size		2 9
5	,,	,,			2 3
6	,,	,,	,,		3 0
7	,,	,,	,, superior		3 6
8	,,	,,	large size		3 3
9	,,	,,	medium size		3 0
10	,,	,,	,,		3 3
11	,,	,,	small size		2 6
12	,,	,,	,, superior		3 0
13	,,	,,	two blades, superior		4 6
14	,,	,,	white handle		1 6
15	**Pruning Knife and Saw**				5 6
16	**Pruning and Budding Knife**				4 6
17	**Budding Knife**, large size				3 6
18	,,	,,	medium size		3 0
19	,,	,,	,, ,, brass capped		4 0
20	,,	,,			4 0
21	,,	,,	medium size		3 0
22	,,	,,	small size		3 0
23	,,	,,	medium size		4 0
24	,,	,,			3 3
25	,,	,,			3 0
26	,,	,,			2 9
27	,,	,,			3 0
28	,,	,,	small size		2 9
29	,,	,,	smallest size		2 0
30	,,	,,	two blades		5 0
31	,,	,,	with scissors, superior		7 6
32	,,	,,	Stag-horn handle, very strong		4 6

No.				Each s. d.
33	**Knife**, with botanical lens			4 0
34	,,	,, two blades		5 0
35	**Gentleman's Pocket Knife**, three blades, superior			5 0
36	,,	,,	Ivory handle, two blades, and scissors	6 0
37	**Gentleman's Pocket Knife**, Pearl handle, two blades, cork-screw, and saw, superior			7 6
38	,,	,, Tortoise-shell handle, two blades		5 6
39	**Lady's Pocket Knife**, Tortoise-shell handle, three blades			5 0
40	,,	Pearl handle, two blades		3 6
41	**Silver Fruit Knife**, Hall-marked, superior quality			7 6
42	,,			5 6
	Tam o' Shanter Hone, for sharpening knives. In wood case			2 6
	,,	,, without case		1 0
43	**Pruning Scissors**, large size			3 0
44	,,	small size		2 6
45	**Flower Gatherer**, large size			4 0
46	,,	small size		3 0
47	**Vine Scissors**			3 0
48	**Propagating Scissors**			2 6
49	**Shred Scissors**			2 6
50	**Sécateurs** (English make) with Nowill's patent screw regulator			6 6
51	,,	,, with spiral spring		5 6
52	,,	,, very powerful		6 6
53	,,	,, for Roses, disbudding Chrys-anthemums, &c., a very use-ful implement		6 6
54	,,	,, 8-inch		5 6
54A	,,	,, 7-inch		5 0
55	**Sécateurs**, or French Pruning Shears, 8½-inch			4 6
55A	,,	,, 7½-inch		4 0
55B	,,	,, 6½-inch		3 6
55C	**Pliers**, combination, for cutting wire &c.			2 9

SUTTON & SONS, Seed Growers and Merchants, READING, ENGLAND.

In 1912 knives, scissors, saws and pruners still constituted a large part of the gardener's armoury. Pruning and budding knives were offered in a multitude of designs and sizes; pruners had become secateurs or French pruning shears, but the basic design remained unchanged from those shown on page 15.

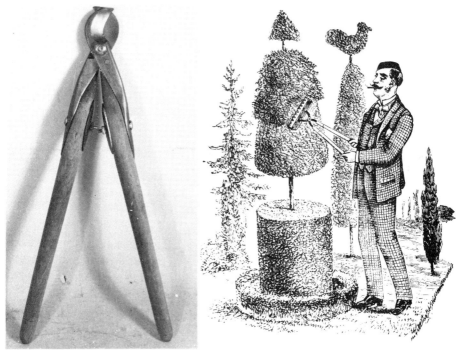

ABOVE LEFT: *Long-handled or parrot-bill pruners. The long handles allowed more leverage so that quite thick branches could be cut. These are still used today.*

ABOVE RIGHT: *Later in the nineteenth century both long-handled and short-handled clippers were available with multiple blades moving in counteraction on the clipper principle.*

BELOW: *From a book of 1777, a metal wheelbarrow, fitted with a grille and shoot at the front to act as a spreader and a wide wheel, useful when gravel was being spread on paths to roll and level at once.*

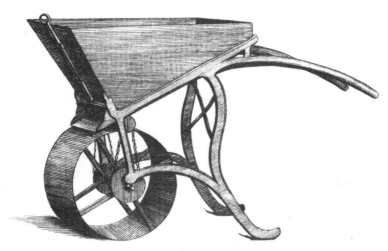

SAMUELSON'S BOYD'S PATENT LAWN MOWING & ROLLING MACHINES.

30-inch wide Pony-Power Machine; made also of smaller sizes for Hand-Power.

SOLE MANUFACTURER, B. SAMUELSON, BRITANNIA WORKS, BANBURY, OXON.

About 1850 both Thomas Green of Leeds and Samuelsons of Banbury began to make a wide mower, around 40 inches (1 metre), designed to be drawn by a pony or donkey. 'As the machine makes little noise', it was claimed, 'the most spirited animal can be employed without fear of it running away.' The pony's feet were dressed in leather overshoes to prevent hoof and shoe marks on the grass. This model became extremely popular and it was reported that the demand was so great that at times the mowers were painted on the train taking them to their destination.

THE LAWN

When Loudon was compiling his various editions of the *Encyclopaedia of Gardening* in the 1820s there were no mechanised garden tools. What tools there were, he says, were 'generally adapted for labour which requires more force than skill, they are generally large and require the use of both hands and the muscular action of the whole frame, often aided by gravity'.

Eighteenth-century lawns were cut with a scythe and a reasonably level sward could be achieved by skilled mowers. An acre (0.4 ha) of lawn required three men to work for a day but, however skilled they were, 'circular sears and inequalities and bare places ... continue for several days' — so wrote Budding in 1830 when he patented the first cylindrical-blade lawn-mower. It was not manufactured until 1832 (although a prototype had been made in 1831 by Farrabee to Budding's design),

when it was patented as the first cylindrical-blade mower. Budding based the design on the rotary blades used in the local cloth industry to achieve a close even pile on high-quality textiles. That first mower had a 19-inch (480 mm) cutting blade which worked against a rigid knife bar on the underside of the machine. The mower was designed to be pushed from the rear but had another handle at the front so that it could be pulled by a second worker in difficult areas. *The Gardener's Magazine* claimed in the 1830s that 'country gentlemen may find in using the machine themselves an amusing, useful and healthy exercise.'

One of the first to be purchased was bought by the Zoological Garden at Regent's Park, London. The machine was bought for ten guineas and the price included a wooden packing case and delivery. (The manufacturer's catalogue

ABOVE AND OPPOSITE: *Details from a series of paintings by Balthazar Nebot. c. 1738. depict gardeners working with tools at Hartwell House, Buckinghamshire (see also pages 3 and 16-17). Lawns were then mown with a scythe, an implement used with both hands and without bending the back. Three skilled mowers could scythe an acre of lawn in a day, but, however accomplished they were circular sears and inequalities were visible in the grass afterwards. Lawns were constantly rolled to render the surface level, to facilitate the operation of scything and reduce the possibility of bare patches of earth being exposed by the scythe blade.*

These paintings can be seen at the Buckinghamshire County Museum in Church Street, Aylesbury, and are of considerable interest because they show the Restoration style of garden design then in fashion.

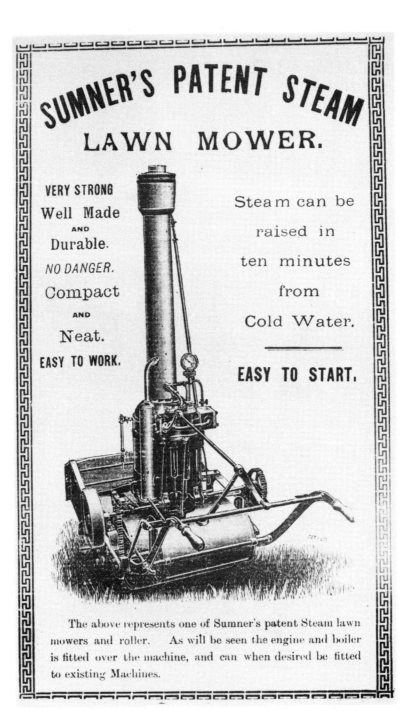

SUMNER'S PATENT STEAM
LAWN MOWER.

VERY STRONG
Well Made
AND
Durable.
NO DANGER.
Compact
AND
Neat.
EASY TO WORK.

Steam can be
raised in
ten minutes
from
Cold Water.

___

EASY TO START.

The above represents one of Sumner's patent Steam lawn mowers and roller. As will be seen the engine and boiler is fitted over the machine, and can when desired be fitted to existing Machines.

ABOVE: *When Alexander Shanks of Arbroath patented his horse- or pony-drawn mower, Queen Victoria was one of his first customers and this advertisement depicts his wares in use on the lawn at Balmoral.*

OPPOSITE: *In 1895 the Lancashire Steam Motor Company of Leyland produced a steam-driven mower, patented by Sumner. It was fired by oil and weighed 1½ tons. The operator walked behind it to guide it. This steam mower, once under way, carried a large grass box at the front. Note the heavy roller to the rear.*

offered package and delivery 'to any principal railway station in the United Kingdom.') In 1832 J. R. & A. Ransome of Ipswich, previously manufacturers of steam engines, were licensed to manufacture the machine.

Ten years before the Great Exhibition of 1851 Alexander Shanks of Arbroath, Scotland, had registered a pony-drawn mower of his own design which also swept up the mowings. About this time Samuelson of Banbury began to manufacture their pony-drawn mowing and rolling machine.

During the middle of the nineteenth century there were various innovations. Barnard, Bishop & Barnard of Norwich introduced a 'noiseless machine' constructed with a rubber tyre and without chains and gear wheels; in the late 1860s a rotary-action leaf sweeper for lawns appeared and in the 1870s lawn edgers were made to trim the well groomed edges of the numerous flowerbeds that dotted the lawns of Victorian gardens.

It was fifty years after the introduction of the mower that grinding machines to sharpen the blade came on the market, as if it was an afterthought to admit that lawnmowers needed to be maintained. After-sales service was introduced by Atco in 1922 and in 1925 the Royal Horticultural Society organised tests — or trials — in Regent's Park, for motor mowers. A few years before the Second World War Power Specialists of Slough introduced the rotary mower Rotoscythe and offered both petrol-driven and electric models.

In the 1960s lightweight electric mowers came on to the market and in 1966 the Flymo was developed by Flymo Ltd of

ABOVE LEFT: *Heavy rollers pulled by two gardeners or by a pony were used long before the nineteenth century. This model, illustrated in 'Descriptions of Some of the Utensils of Husbandry' (1777), shows a divided cast iron roller with decorated handle. Two cylinders revolved independently, making rolling easier and turning simpler. The balance controlled the handle so that once released it swung into the upright position and the roller remained stationary.*
TOP RIGHT: *A light stone roller with wrought iron handle.*
ABOVE RIGHT: *A wooden roller of the late nineteenth century.*

Middlesbrough. It used a rotary action to provide a cushion of air to support the machine.

Rollers of both stone and wood had been used on lawns before the advent of the mowing machine, and during the nineteenth century larger and heavier iron rollers were widely used. Tennis and croquet became popular sports and both these games demanded an even turf. Iron rollers usually had swing handles that could be moved from one side to the other so that the roller could be moved in either direction. Many were made in two sections to facilitate turning, and some were advertised as 'self-cleaning' — there was a bar running across the top of the roller to scrape away the accumulated mud.

The nineteenth - century rollers illustrated would have been used on both lawns and paths. It was often recommended that the operator should wear either light shoes or shoes with low heels when rolling a path so that his footmarks should not spoil the finished effect. Paths were also raked to obliterate footmarks.

ABOVE: *In 1862 John Lampit & Co of Banbury were advertising their leaf sweeper for lawns. No doubt this could also be used for collecting longer grass that was cut by hook or sickle. The machine consisted of a number of brushes and blades which rotated rapidly and, backed by a fan, disturbed and collected the leaves.*

BELOW: *The watering of lawns became a necessity and the Gutta Percha Company produced lengths of tubing, with a union joint every 100 yards (90 metres), for use on lawns. This is one of their advertisements of 1859, but very soon afterwards elaborate jets were available as sprinklers for lawn watering. The jets bore fanciful names and shapes, such as Prince of Wales feathers; but they had to be constantly moved to water anything but the smallest domestic lawn.*

ABOVE LEFT: *An early lawn sprinkler, patented by W. de Normanville, Borough Engineer of Leamington Spa.*

ABOVE LEFT: *Lawn edge cutters which were pushed along seemed preferable to shears or hand clippers in nineteenth-century flower gardens, where there were many flowerbeds of many shapes dotted about the lawns and consequently many yards of edges to be kept trim.*

BELOW: *By 1904 Ransomes of Ipswich produced this magnificent machine with a water-cooled 2¾ horsepower engine. There was also about the same time a splendid model on which the operator could sit, and this enabled the lawn to be mown in less time.*

An early knapsack-type sprayer, c. 1898. The pump is activated by the operator pulling and releasing the handle to build up pressure and force a spray at the nozzle held in the other hand.

GARDEN SUNDRIES

There is written evidence that from the earliest times gardeners have sought to protect plants from winter cold and dampness and have encouraged earlier crops in this way. Glazed hand lights of metal frame in a variety of designs provided such protection and were portable. Bell glasses or 'lettuce growers' were formed of one piece of glass, bell-shaped and with a knob at the top for carrying. These preceded the glazed hand lights. During the 1930s both types were replaced by glass cloches, many of which could be dismantled and stored when not in use.

In the eighteenth century bell glasses were used for a number of kitchen-garden crops, even for melons and cauliflowers, and gardeners were advised to sow seed 'under the edge of the glasses over your cauliflower' to protect them.

Oiled paper was used to form early frames in the eighteenth century, and in the nineteenth century, although glass was then much cheaper, calico soaked in a mixture of boiled linseed oil and soft soap was used to protect frames from dampness. It was the same mixture that sailors used for waterproofing jackets, leggings and caps.

Frames constructed either of boards or a few courses of brickwork were used for raising early salad crops such as radish, carrots and lettuces as well as flowers such as violets. Special varieties of vegetable were recommended for frame culture, far more than they are today. Frames were and are used for housing cuttings and the like.

Wire mesh of varying weight and mesh size was widely used in the garden before the advent of plastics. As fencing and as tennis-court boundary netting it still is used to some extent. Pea guards were used just as a modern plastic cloche is used to

29

ABOVE: *Two bell glasses, used to protect plants from cold and wet weather and so encourage earlier crops, and (centre) an early garden frame covered in oiled paper, used to similar effect.*

OPPOSITE: *A manufacturer's advertisement. At the left of the second row is a frame with glazed lights. The lights slotted into grooves and could be pulled back to control ventilation. Bottom left is a gauze box frame, the lid of which was hinged to give extra ventilation when required. Called a plant preserver, it would afford only slight protection from the weather but good protection from birds and rabbits. Similar wire mesh was used for fencing (centre top and bottom, and third row, right). All types of plant supports (top left and second row, right) and pea guards (bottom right) were available, and also shown are a water barrow and a pneumatic-tyred wheelbarrow.*

protect seedlings but if not removed in time became a horrible tangle of pea haulms. Ultimately the metalwork rusted and had to be scraped with a wire brush and even dipped and sprayed with insecticide.

An immense range of metal plant supports was obtainable, including wires stretched along walls, with wall eyes for guiding the wires and so-called 'radiseurs' for tightening the wires at each end. These wires were (and still are) used for training fruit trees and decorative climbing plants on a wall. Climbing plants, notably roses, were also supported by arches and a variety of shapes and sizes was available.

Watering has always been a vital operation in plant cultivation of any kind. Water pots used to be of clay and resembled coffee pots in size and shape, but in the nineteenth century, when metal cans could be shaped, they were larger with open necks and could be made in varying sizes. Many of them were 'japanned', which meant that they were given the appearance of having been polished with blacking. When galvanising

came into common use there was no longer a need for this high-quality finish. The rose has been used for 'dewing the seedlings' since very early days. The nineteenth century brought a wide choice of shapes and sizes of water pots for use both in the conservatory and outdoors; the spouts were sometimes interchangeable to give some control over the rate at which water flowed. The zigzag spout, for example, stemmed the flow of water with considerable precision.

On a large scale, mobile galvanised water carts, also called water machines, were used for carrying water into the garden so that a watering can could be dipped into it and filled repeatedly. Some carts tipped easily so that most of the water could be removed in this way. Alternatively the carts were fitted with a syringe and pressure could be obtained to produce a spray for use with insecticide or fungicide. Such preparations would be of soft soap, naphthalene or copper sulphide (Bordeaux mixture) and were mixed in the cart itself with a given proportion of water. Because the barrel

BARNARDS LIMITED, NORWICH, England

ESTABLISHED 1826

"Norvic" Chain Link Fencing for all Purposes—
Estate, Garden, Dog Enclosures, &c.

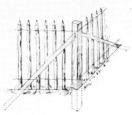

Chestnut Pale Fencing, well made,
good materials. Produced by ex-service
men in the Forest of Dean.

Garden Arches and Espaliers.

Garden Frames for all purposes.
Violet Frames, Plants, &c.

New Article—Garden Barrow with
Pneumatic Balloon Tyre. The most
useful Barrow yet introduced.

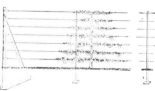

Specialists in Espalier Work of all kinds.

Water Barrows of all types to
suit all purposes.

Prices reduced.

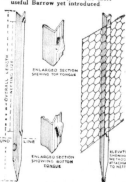

ENLARGED SECTION
SHEWING TOP TONGUE

ENLARGED SECTION
SHOWING BOTTOM
TONGUE

ELEVATION
SHOWING
METHOD OF
ATTACHMENT
TO NETTING

The new Garden Stake No. 611.
The cheapest and most
adaptable Stake yet
introduced.

Write for prices, &c..

Inquiries Invited.

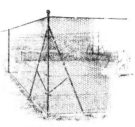

Tennis Court Fencing for all positions and
of every description.

Prices reduced for this season.

Plant Preserver and Rearer for Seedlings.

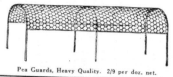

Pea Guards, Heavy Quality. 2/9 per doz. net.

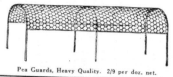

London Office :
110 CANNON STREET, E.C.
Telegrams : Phone :
Barnards Cannon London. Mansion House 8597

Head Office & Works :
NORWICH, ENGLAND
Telegrams : Phone :
Barnards Norwich. 1477 Norwich.

Birmingham Office & Warehouse :
8 Crescent, Cambridge St.
Telegrams : Phone :
Busibee Birmingham. Birmingham Midland 6299

(82

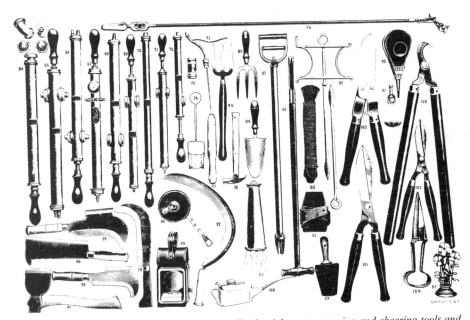

An illustration from a manufacturer's catalogue. To the right, more pruning and shearing tools and across the top an elegant flower gatherer, which not only cuts but holds the bloom otherwise out of reach. The cane handle, 4 feet (1.2 metres) in length, ensured lightness. Below left, an array of billhooks, slashers and hatchets. Above left, a range of syringes. Some were claimed to be specially for use in the greenhouse; others were specially light; others had two or three jets. All these were of brass or nickel-plated and varied in capacity and fineness of spray. They were used for insecticides. Further variations in the war against insects were hand bellows (top right) and a 'puffer' or tobacco powder distributor (top right). Centre left, next to the range of syringes, is an aphis brush, which is in effect a pair of brushes on tongues, allowing the brushes to clear both sides of a leaf or stem simultaneously. Below centre, a so-called sulphurator or 'boite a houppe' (tassel box), which served to dust the plants with flowers of sulphur as a fungicide. The powder was contained in the box itself, the tassel serving to distribute it over the plants — a precursor of the aerosol.

tipped, it could be cleared and washed out after use.

All the sundries illustrated above were generally available in the years immediately before the First World War, but from 1922 to about 1935 the increase in garden appliances and tools reached its peak and 'the right tool for the job' was of the utmost importance. Since the Second World War there has been a swing away from variety of design, mainly because manufactured tools need to be standardised if production is to be economic, and the trend has been towards lightness and ease of manipulation.